THE HEART OF A
GOD FEARING
Woman
Devotional & Journal

LASHAUNDA DICKENSON SKIPPINGS

The Heart of a God Fearing Woman
Devotional & Journal

Copyright © 2023 Lashaunda Skippings
All Rights Reserved.

ISBN 979-8-9865071-0-1

Editor:
Lashaunda Dickenson Skippings

Proofreader:
Patronella Been and Mikilah Forde

Writing Coach:
Robin Cox Foster

Front Cover Design:
Beyond.lc by Oniel Wright

Interior Layout & Design and Cover Layout:
Tarsha L. Campbell

Published by:
DOMINIONHOUSE
Publishing & Design, LLC
P.O. Box 681938 | Orlando, Florida 32868 | 407.703.4800 phone
www.mydominionhouse.com

Dedication

I wrote this devotional with the inspiration of the Holy Spirit as I weathered several storms during my young Christian walk. I am eternally grateful to God for His faithfulness. I was mentored by Apostle Muriel Elaine Harris, a phenomenal woman of God with a selfless devotion to God's people. The poem below was written as a tribute after she passed away on August 9th 2021. She left an indelible mark on my heart and I'm appreciative to have benefited from such wise counsel.

***

Not Another One

There's not another one like you,
Whose smile and laugh triggers everyone else's too.
Who talks for hours to mend and build,
Uplifting Godly spirits within.

There's not another one like you,
Whose faith and trust revealed dumbfounded views.
There's not another one like you,
After a stern rebuke, love was next in cue.
You never held a grudge or showed indifference,
But reminded us often "God don't wink at ignorance!"

There's not another one like you,
To pray us back in line like you do.
"No peace, no rest till you harken to God's voice"
You drilled and prayed till we made the right choice.
"Obedience is better than sacrifice" you would remind
"The recording Angel is taking note all the time".

God must have assigned you management duties up there,
You were a force on earth, sharing His divine love and cheer.

Your work is done our Angel, of this we all are sure,
We'll miss you but can't help but picture, the huge and fluffy
diamond wings
God must have saved for your reward.

Love Always,
Lashaunda Skippings

Acknowledgements

With a heart of gratitude, I express profound thanks to my husband, children, parents, close relatives, my Apostle Clayton Harris and my sisters and brothers of Firm Foundation Ministries International. They have all been instrumental in supporting and holding me accountable in my walk with God. For this I am indeed grateful.

My Elder and cousin Patronella Been assisted in proofreading and editing my first draft. My Elder was an in-depth teacher of God's word with a fine eye for language. She sifted every entry and made corrections and recommendations through God's leading.

Elder Been experienced God's miracle working power first hand and had numerous testimonies of the goodness of God. I am thankful for her selflessness and devotion to Ministry. May she continue to rest in the arms of our Saviour.

"The Lord is my strength and my shield;

my heart trusted in him, and I am

helped: therefore, my heart

greatly rejoiceth; and with

my song will I praise him."

Psalm 28:7 (KJV)

Table of Contents

Table of Contents

"...Then I said, 'Behold, I have come— In the volume of the book it is written of Me— To do Your will, O God.' "

Hebrews 10:7 (NKJV)

"O taste and see that the Lord is good:

blessed is the man that trusteth in him.

O fear the Lord, ye his saints: for there is

no want to them that fear him."

Psalm 34:8-9 (KJV)

Introduction

The Heart of a
God-Fearing Woman

A devotional written from a supernatural collection of experiences that expose the lessons I learned as a new believer in Christ, encountering trials that have had a divine impact on my marriage, family and ministry.

If you are a woman of God or a new believer, the words in this book can have a marvelous influence on your marriage, family and ministry as well. After all, as stewards in Christ we are tasked with being our brother's keeper. Therefore, our testimonies can help to light the way for others if we make known the goodness and faithfulness of God throughout the changing scenes of life.

"Our Heavenly Father has never been defeated. He works all things out for your good. Be still and trust Him."

Chapter 1

God Will Fight for You, You Need Only Be Still

Have you ever felt like you were a part of a losing team, or have you felt defeated after doing things the right way and doing your utmost best?

This is the way it feels at times when we are at war with the enemy. In these times we must remember that greater is He that is within us than he that is within the world. Just like David, a child... going to battle with a giant, to the natural eye the child is already defeated. However, God was on his side. No matter how it looks or how hard the battle gets as long as we obey God and live upright and in alignment with His word, He will fight for us. We need only be still. He is Jehovah Gibbor. He is the Lion of the Tribe of Judah, Mighty in Battle! He has overcome the world for our sake. Stand back and allow Him to fight your battles.

He's the God that kept Daniel, Shadrach, Meshach and Abednego, He's the God that delivered the Israelites, the covenant keeping God of Abraham, Isaac and Jacob. He is ever present, alive and able to win every battle you commit to Him. Trust Him, nothing is too hard for Him and nothing is impossible with Him. Do not look at what you can see with the natural eye but know that your Heavenly Father has never been defeated. He works all things out for your good. Be still and trust Him.

"Ye shall not need to fight in this battle: set yourselves,
stand ye still, and see the salvation of the Lord with you."
2 Chronicles 20:17

"The Lord shall fight for you,
and ye shall hold your peace."
Exodus 14:14 (KJV)

What the Spirit of the Lord spoke to my heart

_____

_____

_____

_____

_____

_____

_____

_____

_____

_____

_____

_____

_____

_____

_____

_____

"God's word is a timely reminder that

we are valuable. If He feeds the fowls

of the air and looks about the lilies

how much more would

He regard His children?"

Chapter 2

Words Are Powerful

———

The saying "sticks and stones may break my bones but words will never hurt me" is just a mere chant we learn as a coping skill growing up. It helped us to deal with bullying and verbal abuse. As we get older the effects of words cut more deeply than they did before, especially when it comes from someone you love. But what if we shift our focus to what God says about us? What if we remind ourselves that we are fearfully and wonderfully made, in Gods image and for His purpose and glory? God declared that He wishes above all things that we prosper and be in good health, He declares in His word that we are the apple of His eye. His word reminds us that we are children of the King!

Our Heavenly Father spoke this entire universe into existence using His words. Imagine how transformational His promises can be to your life when you begin to repeat them and remind yourself of who you are in His eyes and who's you are. God promises to provide all our needs according to His riches in glory. His word reminds us that we can do all things through Him who strengthens us. It reminds us that promotion is from above, and that man makes plans but it is the counsel of the Lord that prevails.

God's word is a timely reminder that we are valuable. If He feeds the fowls of the air and looks about the lilies how much more would He regard His children?

In times of doubt and depression caused by the sharp snares of someone's words, be reminded to see your self the way your Heavenly Father sees you. As a child of the King, fearfully and wonderfully made in His image and for His glory!

"For you created my inmost being; you knit me together in my mother's womb. I praise you because I am fearfully and wonderfully made; your works are wonderful, I know that full well."
Psalms 139:13-14

What the Spirit of the Lord spoke to my heart

_____

_____

_____

_____

_____

_____

_____

_____

_____

_____

_____

_____

_____

_____

_____

"Get into a posture of prayer to fight

your battles. Remember that your

God is mighty in battle,

and He cannot lose."

Chapter 3

Though Cast Down,
You Are Not Defeated

———

The enemy's plan is to steal, kill and destroy. It never changes, he has the same aim and same old tricks. If the enemy can succeed at attacking your mind, stealing your joy, and destroying your confidence, then he has killed you. God has given us dominion over this earth, he has equipped us with all that we need for battle. Why battle? Because we cannot allow the enemy to steal, destroy and kill what is not his. We must take back, with force, everything that God has given to us; our joy, peace and sanity were all gifts from God.

Get up! "Let not your heart be troubled neither let it be afraid". Do not let fear overtake you, do not allow yourself to feel defeated. Do not lay waste while the enemy walks off with your belongings.

Our Jehovah Gibbor is mighty in battle, He declared that the weapons of our warfare are not carnal, but mighty. Trust Him today and use your God given power to overcome the snares of the enemy. Get into a posture of prayer to fight your battles. Remember that your God is mighty in battle, and He cannot lose. Do not be deceived by what you see in the natural for there is greater in store for those that trust and fear the Lord and those that keep His statutes.

"Finally, my brethren, be strong in the Lord, and in the power of his might. Put on the whole armour of God, that ye may be able to stand against the wiles of the devil."
Ephesians 6:10-11

What the Spirit of the Lord spoke to my heart

_____

_____

_____

_____

_____

_____

_____

_____

_____

_____

_____

_____

_____

_____

_____

"If you want to see God move in miraculous ways you must submit to His will and allow Him to shape and lead you."

Chapter 4

Understanding
Your Valley

———

Alone, short changed, defeated, empty, drained, torn, broken, misunderstood, hopeless? .... If you feel any of these traits, you may feel that God has forsaken you or forgotten about you. It is important that although you may have sunken deep in distress or into misery that you take a minute to reflect and understand the reason for being on the crossroad you are at in life.

The trials you face could be because of your own irresponsible decision making. It could be that you are undergoing attacks from the enemy, or it could be the will of God that you face tribulations so that your life is shaped to bring about God's divine purpose.

A time of reflection will reveal to you the purpose for your valley. Regardless of why you are tried, the Bible reassures us that we can have peace and rest in God. The Bible declares that all things work together for the good of those that love the Lord and are called according to His purpose.

Repenting, surrendering and wholeheartedly giving over your entire being would feel like a sacrifice of your life but it is exactly where you need to be for God to move on your behalf. If you want to see God move in miraculous ways you must submit to His will and allow Him to shape and lead you. God chastises those He loves, but He promises that though you may be heavily afflicted He will deliver you from it all.

How should you now move forward?

- If it is that you are at the root of your own problems. You may not have taken heed to the call of God on your life. You may know God's plan for you well, but you want to delay it until you get yourself together, or until you are done with 'living your best young life'. The problem here is that you are on God's timing, not your own. Your days are borrowed, and tomorrow is not promised to you. You must decide whether to be of the world or of the Lord. Keep your hands and your hearts clean. Your God is a healer, your God is a provider, your God is a comforter, He is a friend to the friendless and a father to the fatherless. He is everything you need him to be. You need only to surrender your ways to Him and trust Him to lead you as you walk upright. Allow God to work in your life, take your hands off the wheel and be an obedient follower. Do not be a speaker and a hearer of the word, be a doer. Be obedient to the call of God on your life and allow Him to lead you as He sees fit, according to His will, His purpose and His plan for you.

Finally, the Bible reminds us to study to show ourselves approved. Immerse yourself in the word of God, trust and believe in the word of God, hide it in your heart that you may not sin against Him. Allow it to be a lamp unto your feet and a light unto your path. As you turn your life around and live as your Heavenly Father intended, watch Him begin to move in your life and work everything together for your good.

- All hell may be breaking loose in your life because you are under the attack of the enemy but remember that your God is mighty in battle. The Bible declares that there is nothing too hard for him. His word teaches us how to pray and assures us that the weapons of our warfare are not carnal but mighty to the pulling down of strong holds. Be mindful that "we wrestle not against flesh and blood, but against principalities, against powers, against the rulers of the darkness of this world, against spiritual wickedness in high places." The word of God commands "Wherefore take unto you the whole armour of God, that ye may be able to withstand in the evil day, and having done all, to stand." Persistence in prayer, faithful service, righteous living, and our sword which is the word of God are the key tools we need to claim victory already afforded to us over the enemy through Christ Jesus.

- Speak his promises over your life. Speak greatness over your life and over your children. We easily speak curses through silly sayings and things we think are funny. We sing songs and repeat chants that attract evil spirits then we wonder why we are dismayed or heartbroken.

The Bible declares that life and death are in the power of the tongue. We can speak things into existence, and we should not take lightly the things we continually repeat because they can become open declarations that the enemy will use to overcome us. Refrain from negative speech and speak life, for your words are powerful, even in the simplest conversations. Declare that your mind is at peace in Christ Jesus. Do not claim stress, misery, sickness or defeat but remind yourself that you are a child of the Most High God! You were made in His image and for His glory. The word of God declares that He will provide all of your needs according to his riches in glory. Remember that weeping endures for a night, but joy comes in the morning. Remind yourself that you can do all things through Christ who strengthens you. Remind yourself that all things work together for the good of those that love the Lord and are called according to His perfect plan! We are His workmanship and He regards us higher than the birds of the air that He feeds and the lilies of the valleys that He clothes in beauty. Also think

this way and speak this way of yourself, declare
only the blessings of God over your life.

*"My son do not make light of the Lord's discipline, and do not
lose heart when he rebukes you, because the Lord disciplines
the one he loves and he chastens everyone
he accepts as his son."*
Hebrews 12:5-6

*"If you say, "the Lord is my refuge" and you make the Most
High your dwelling, no harm will overtake you, no disaster
will come near your tent. For he will command his angels
concerning you to guard you in all your ways;
they will lift you up in their hands so that
you will not strike your foot against a stone."*
Psalms 91:9-12

*"The tongue has the power of life and death, and those who
love it will eat its fruit."*
Proverbs 18:21

What the Spirit of the Lord spoke to my heart

_____

_____

_____

_____

_____

_____

_____

_____

_____

_____

_____

_____

_____

_____

"If you consult with God and ask Him to lead the way, take your hand off the wheel and trust Him to take over and bring about His will for your life."

Chapter 5

Get Out of Your Own Way!

———

Often as saints we pray for God's intervention, for His guidance and for His blessing but still we try doing things in our own strength making decisions that we think are safe, that are logical and makes sense to us.

The thing is, God's ways are far from those of man and in order to receive an extraordinary blessing from Him we have to take our mind off of what we can see with the naked eye and be open to allowing God to direct us through our faith in His word.

The Bible says not to look at what you can see because those things are temporal but rather to look at what you can't see which is eternal.

"Now faith is the substance of things hoped for, the evidence of things not seen." Hebrews 11:1 KJV

This is simply nudging you to see things through your spiritual eyes with faith in God and His promises, trusting that He will make all things perfect concerning you.

Do not try to find your way in your own strength, do not hold back a monetary seed the Holy Spirit has lead you to give because it was set aside for something else or because it was your last. Do not hold on to something God is removing from your life to position you for better, do not ignore a task because you think you are not capable.

If you consult with God and ask Him to lead the way, take your hand off the wheel and trust Him to take over and bring about His will for your life. Allow Him to prove Himself as your Saviour, allow Him to show up strong. Surrender your ways to Him and trust that His way is best.

"Trust in the Lord with all thine heart; and lean not unto thine own understanding. In all thy ways acknowledge him, and he shall direct thy paths."
Proverbs 3:5-6

What the Spirit of the Lord spoke to my heart

_____

_____

_____

_____

_____

_____

_____

_____

_____

_____

_____

_____

_____

_____

_____

"Once we keep our minds on Him he

promised to keep us in perfect peace.

He said he will perfect everything

concerning us, he promised

that all things would work

together for our good."

Chapter 6

Be Obedient to the Voice of God

———

In the parable of the dragnet, Jesus uses a simple story to teach us of the blessings that obedience yields. In the same way with our lives, we must be quick to obey the voice of God. It is a privilege to be commanded by God. Not many people are able to hear God's voice, if He speaks to you be quick to listen and follow His commands. The Bible reminds us that obedience is better than sacrifice. There are times when God may direct us along a path that we believe does not make sense. Be obedient anyway and be reminded that His ways are not like ours. What He does is well done. If we love God, believe in Him and trust Him, we should be quick to harken unto His word.

When we begin to walk in the path which He directs He will make the way clear, straight and smooth we need only to trust and obey. It is then our hearts will be filled with peace and joy. He will equip us with what is needed for the journey He has set us on. Once we keep our minds on Him, He promised to keep us in perfect peace. He said He will perfect everything concerning us, He promised that all things would work together for our good.

Our experiences in the tough times cause us to know the goodness of our God having experienced Him moving in wondrous ways. Therefore being obedient brings a feeling of contentment rather then sacrifice as we walk by faith leaning on the Lord.

"The people that know their God are strong people
and they do exploits."
Daniel 11:32

What the Spirit of the Lord spoke to my heart

_____

_____

_____

_____

_____

_____

_____

_____

_____

_____

_____

_____

_____

_____

_____

_____

"In these times we must get out of our own way to understand what God's purpose really is. Most times it is much bigger than what we can perceive."

Chapter 7

Obedience

———

In every story in the Bible, God's people were tested and tried by Him. When the Israelites were freed and began their journey in the wilderness, we learn that their behaviour in the wilderness was the reason why they travailed so long. Had they trusted God completely and kept obedient to His teachings through Moses, their test may not have lasted 40 years.

It is paramount therefore to be obedient to God's voice and His instructions through His prophets. In biblical days and still today, God directs His people according to His purpose for their lives. For them to be gifted and blessed in abundance, their worthiness is tested and tried. If He can trust us with little, He will bless us with much.

Not only does God test us before He blesses us, He also takes us through experiences in order to elevate us. Sometimes what we go through may feel like a total sacrifice of our lives and you wonder, why me? When will it end? Has God forgotten me? Am I worthy of deliverance? In these times we must get out of our own way to understand what God's purpose really is. Most times it is much bigger than what we can perceive. God builds ministries through a faithful few people who lay down their lives and choose to trust Him and obey His every command regardless of the circumstances, regardless of the noise in the market, and regardless of how much of yourself you lose in the process.

The aim is to ultimately lose sight of your flesh and work towards spiritual goals ordained by God in His time, and at His pace. This requires us as believers to trust what we can't understand, have faith in His promises to us and completely obey Him regardless of not being cognizant of the basis of His commands or weighing how silly the commands may seem to the natural eye.

Souls and kingdom work become trapped and held up when we chose to do things our way. We hold back our own deliverance and blessings, we hinder our prayers from being heard when we hesitate to obey because we feel that the command or instruction doesn't make sense. In fact it's not to be understood in the instant we get it. It's to be obeyed. Just like an instruction from a stern Caribbean parent; when you didn't understand the reasoning behind the commands as a child, you asked "why?" The response you got was; "because I say so!" Who are you as a child to answer back or disobey? In the same way we must humble ourselves always and see ourselves as children of our Heavenly Father. Who are we to ask why? Who are we to not obey?

If there were repercussions in the Caribbean household, there are repercussions when we don't obey our Heavenly Father.

Do not stifle your elevation, block your blessing, delay your deliverance, or hinder salvation for the souls of God's people by choosing to be disobedient. Humble yourselves under the command of your Heavenly Father.

"And Samuel said, Hath the Lord as great delight in burnt offerings and sacrifices, as in obeying the voice of the Lord? Behold, to obey is better than sacrifice, and to hearken than the fat of rams."
1 Samuel 15:22

What the Spirit of the Lord spoke to my heart

_____

_____

_____

_____

_____

_____

_____

_____

_____

_____

_____

_____

_____

_____

_____

What the Spirit of the Lord spoke to my heart

_____

_____

_____

_____

_____

_____

_____

_____

_____

_____

_____

_____

_____

_____

"God can help us to steer through what may seem as simple as making a decision on what to have for lunch or where to park at work."

Chapter 8

Consult with God First

———

The Bible gives us a powerful reminder in Philippians 4: 6-7:

"Be careful for nothing; but in every thing by prayer and supplication with thanksgiving let your requests be made known unto God. And the peace of God, which passeth all understanding, shall keep your hearts and minds through Christ Jesus."

There are many times we leave an argument, conversation or meeting that takes a turn for the worst just because of words spoken. There are times we make decisions that we cannot change, there are times we are uncertain about how to approach situations and have regrets afterwards.

No matter how simple, if you are dealing with a relationship, a plan, an idea or a decision, take a quick moment to ask

God's covering over your mind. His word reminds us that He gives wisdom when we ask of Him.

God can and wants to help us to steer through what may seem as simple as making a decision on what to have for lunch or where to park at work. By committing our thoughts to His obedience and humbling ourselves to always be led by his Holy Spirit we can avoid what could result in an upset stomach or an issue of a hit and run in the parking lot.

It begins with surrendering your very being to be in alignment with God's will daily, allowing Him to lead you through His word and by His Holy Spirit.

Intentionally seeking God before decision making, meetings, discussions or even conversations can bring about a totally different outcome than when we are led by our emotions or sometimes pride. We must trust God and remember that He knows best, and His purpose is to give us hope, a future and an expected end.

What the Spirit of the Lord spoke to my heart

_____

_____

_____

_____

_____

_____

_____

_____

_____

_____

_____

_____

_____

_____

"For us to be at peace and live long, happy and fulfilling lives we must seek God first and be sure that we do not lose sight of our divine purpose or our relationship with Him."

Chapter 9

Keep Your Eyes on God He Will Establish You in Due Time

———

The Bible tells us to take no worry for what we will eat or what we will wear. For our Heavenly Father feeds the fowls of the air and considers even the lilies. He knows all that we are in need of and regards us higher than the birds, lilies and grass. He commands us, "*Seek ye first the kingdom of God, and his righteousness; and all these things shall be added unto you.*" - Matthew 6:33

We live in an era now where there is a fight to be on top and a race to be wealthy. Everyone's main concern is securing the 'bag'. Very few people are concerned about the ministry of God's word. Very few stop to sacrifice their time for a relationship with Him. There is nothing wrong with having ambition, being strong willed and working hard. The issue is that in most instances God is left out of the equation or He receives what is left of us after we have hustled and bustled for the week. If this is the way you are living, you are living backward.

The Bible reminds us that only what we do for Christ will last. Therefore, after sacrificing time and energy on success, it can all be taken away in the blink of an eye or left behind for someone else to enjoy as a result of death.

God wants us to delight in His work, to build up ourselves spiritually and maintain a close relationship with Him. His word declares that He is a rewarder of those that diligently seek Him. The Bible reminds us over and over to keep God as the head of our lives. He says in all our ways acknowledge Him and He will direct our path.

For us to be at peace and live long, happy and fulfilling lives we must seek God first and be sure that we do not lose sight of our divine purpose or our relationship with Him. Then, He will establish us and prosper us. I'm not telling you not to make business plans or not to go to school or be ambitious. I am admonishing you not to let these things have more precedence over your relationship with God and your spiritual walk. Be sure that all you do is in accordance with God's word and His purpose for your life.

As long as you are walking upright, He will allow everything to fall into place for you, success, love, peace, finance, health, strength... these will all be afforded to you as His blessings.

Being intentional and firm in your walk with Him will establish you in His kingdom and on earth. You will be able to ask anything in His name. You will be able to withstand all darts of the enemy and ultimately rise above your fears. All His promises and plans will be made available to you. At the end of this life, you would have enjoyed His riches on earth and moved on to do the same in heaven. Therefore, joy, peace and blessings will be attached to your name and lined up for your seed.

"Trust in the Lord, and do good; so shalt thou dwell in the land, and verily thou shalt be fed. Delight thyself also in the Lord; and he shall give thee the desires of thine heart. Commit thy way unto the Lord; trust also in him; and he shall bring it to pass."
Psalms 37:3-5

What the Spirit of the Lord spoke to my heart

_____

_____

_____

_____

_____

_____

_____

_____

_____

_____

_____

_____

_____

_____

What the Spirit of the Lord spoke to my heart

"The proud are not open to rebuke and often are blinded towards the ways of God. Their hearts are hardened because they do not openly allow themselves to feel and experience trials and testing."

Chapter 10

The Road to Humility

———

O ften times we face many trials in our lives that turn out to be the foundation of our purpose. The Bible declares that tribulation worketh patience; patience > experience; experience> hope: and hope maketh not ashamed.

It is with the overcoming of our trials that we grow spiritually and are worthy of receiving our blessings. However, during our struggles we are instructed to trust God and lean on His word. His word instructs us to put on a garment of praise for the spirit of heaviness. We are to be thankful and prayerful even in our valleys.

It takes a pure heart to be able to humble yourself before the Lord and still trust in Him no matter how dark your circumstances. The Lord despises pride. He looks for those who are humble in spirit to use and to bless.

The proud are not open to rebuke and often are blinded towards the ways of God. Their hearts are hardened because they do not openly allow themselves to feel and experience trials and testing. Therefore, they are not able to appreciate and understand the lessons attached.

After being tested and tried, God's purpose for us as believers is to acquire the fruits of the spirit, love, joy, peace, long suffering, gentleness, goodness, faith, meekness and temperance.

Looking through the natural eye or through vain sight, we may see ourselves as good people. Although we may have good traits and may be living the best we can, we encounter trials in life to perfect our gifts and to grow closer to our Heavenly Father in spirit. He desires that we put our flesh under subjection and walk and live being led by the Holy Spirit.

"Humble yourselves therefore under the mighty hand of God, that he may exalt you in due time."
1 Peter 5:6

What the Spirit of the Lord spoke to my heart

_____

_____

_____

_____

_____

_____

_____

_____

_____

_____

_____

_____

_____

_____

"Continue serving God in spirit and in truth, continue to cry out and seek His face for not only yourself but others that He may allow to cross your paths."

Chapter 11

Do Not Be Distracted, Stay Connected

———

It is so common that after God blesses us and aligns all that we have been praying for, we become slack in our service, lazy in our prayer life and comfortable in our praise. We lose the 'heart' that we put into worshipping. The same 'heart' was awarded to us when we cried out in the midst of our valleys. We cease weeping and wailing because there's no more pain... we begin to pick up old habits and behaviors and forget the things and the ways of God.

We see Him now as great and mighty in giving, graceful and merciful but forget that He is also a God of correction and that He is a jealous God.

Our valleys or conditions were indeed the force that led us to the straight and narrow path of righteousness through much prayer and supplication. Do not only remember your Savior in times of trouble, be just as radical in worship and prayer when everything is aligned as you were when your life was in shambles.

Continue serving God in spirit and in truth, continue to cry out and seek His face for not only yourself but others that He may allow to cross your paths. Testify and share of His goodness so that men may be led to repentance. Never give up or let go of God, He promises to never leave you nor forsake you. The Bible declares that if you make your bed in hell He will be there. Hold on to the unchanging hand of our gracious Father. There is nothing the world can offer that is sweeter than the love of God. Do not allow your lights to go dim, do not back burner your service to the one that showed up for you like no other.

"I tell you," He replied, *"if they keep quiet,*
the stones will cry out."
Luke 19:40

What the Spirit of the Lord spoke to my heart

_____

_____

_____

_____

_____

_____

_____

_____

_____

_____

_____

_____

_____

_____

"When we begin to lose sight of what is

wrong in our lives and focus on serving

God, things begin to fall into place

and sometimes more than

we even prayed for."

Chapter 12

Stay Grounded
Despite the Wait

———

V alley experiences tend to leave us feeling drained, defeated and incapable. We are reminded over and over in the Bible to have faith in God's promises, to stand on His word and to trust in Him.

The Bible tells us that when we pray we are to see things as if they are already done, it reminds us to keep our eyes steered upward towards heaven and our minds on the things of God that He may keep our hearts and minds in peace, and that He may perfect everything concerning us. Sometimes it takes years to begin to see God's hand at work, for the children of Israel it took 40 years.

In our waiting it is easy to doubt God, to question His promises and plans, to pick up old habits and to think that He has forgotten about us or is pre-occupied with better things. Don't be deceived, don't be distracted, stay grounded and trust God. These are ways that prolong our breakthrough rather than get God's attention. To invoke the presence of God we must engulf ourselves in a righteous way of life. The Bible says we must be transformed by the renewing of our minds that we may prove what is the good, acceptable, and perfect will of God.

God's word reminds us that if we draw nigh to Him then He will draw nigh to us. We can draw closer to Him through His word, through worship, prayer and acts of service.

To reap a good harvest, time and attention must be given to your crop. You must prioritize cultivating them. In raising children we must also prepare our minds and hearts to love, nurture and most times sacrifice so that our children have what they need in life for happiness, safety, and healthy development. In our professions, we study and work hard for recognition, raises or promotions. In the same way, we must prioritize our relationship with our Heavenly Father that we may grow to know Him better daily, that we may excel spiritually and let our lights shine so that all may see our Father's good work within us. When we begin to lose sight of what is wrong in our lives and focus on serving God things begin to fall into place and sometimes more than we even prayed for.

There is power in waiting, you will begin to notice changes in your attitude and way of life. Often times it is while we wait that we develop, patience, gentleness, kindness, faithfulness, love, joy, peace, goodness and self control. God changes us from within and make us worthy and ready for every good blessing. Hold on to faith and wait, for there is much purpose in our waiting.

"But they that wait upon the Lord shall renew their strength; they shall mount up with wings like eagles; they shall run, and not be weary; and they shall walk, and not faint."
Isaiah 40:31

"Let us hold unswervingly to the hope we profess, for He who promised is faithful."
Hebrews 10:23

"The Lord is not slow in keeping his promise, as some understand slowness. Instead, He is patient with you, not wanting anyone to perish, but everyone to come to repentance."
2 Peter 9:3

What the Spirit of the Lord spoke to my heart

_____

_____

_____

_____

_____

_____

_____

_____

_____

_____

_____

_____

_____

_____

_____

_____

What the Spirit of the Lord spoke to my heart

_____

_____

_____

_____

_____

_____

_____

_____

_____

_____

_____

_____

_____

_____

_____

"Remember we were created in His image for His glory. Our being should honor Him and bring glory to His name as we strive to live by the teachings in His Word no matter how rough the test."

Chapter 13

His Purpose vs Your Plan

———

It's tough coming to the realization that your life is not your own but it's ultimately borrowed time in which you are to complete kingdom assignments.

After getting over the emotions you feel in sacrificing your entire being and what you cooked up as standards and lifetime goals, you are to then focus on your divine purpose in service to our Heavenly Father.

All things concerning you will fall into place as soon as you lose yourself in your restructured goal of pleasing God first and honoring Him with the fruit of your being.

Remember we were created in His image for His glory. Our being should honor Him and bring glory to His name as we strive to live by the teachings in His Word no matter how rough the test.

"But seek first the kingdom of God, and His righteousness,
and all these things shall be added unto you."
Matthew 6:33

"The earth is the Lord's, and everything in it, the world, and
all who live in it; for He founded it on the seas and established
it on the waters. Who may ascend the mountain of the Lord?
Who may stand in his holy place? The one who has clean
hands and a pure heart, who does not trust in an idol or
swear by a false god. They will receive blessing from the Lord
and vindication from God their Savior. Such is the generation
of those who seek Him, who seek your face, God of Jacob."
Psalm 24:3-5

"You may say to yourself, "My power and the strength of
my hands have produced this wealth for me." But remember
the Lord your God, for it is He who gives you the ability to
produce wealth, and so confirms His covenant, which He
swore to your ancestors, as it is today. If you ever forget the
Lord your God and follow other gods and worship
and bow down to them, I testify against you today
that you will surely be destroyed."
Deuteronomy 8:17-19

What the Spirit of the Lord spoke to my heart

_____

_____

_____

_____

_____

_____

_____

_____

_____

_____

_____

_____

_____

_____

_____

_____

"God equips us with wise counsel so that we don't fall prey to the enemy or become a victim of unbelief, deceit or doubt when our minds are crowded."

Chapter 14

Seek Wise Counsel

————

"Hear counsel, and receive instruction, that thou mayest be wise in thy latter end."

As women we have a tendency to vent when we are overwhelmed with what life throws at us, whether it's to a family member, a trusted friend, or our spouse. It could even be to the very next person with whom we come into contact. The best coping skill to practice in weathering life's storms is to stand on Christ who promises to be our Solid Rock. Venting to God in prayer and laying out every burden at the foot of the cross is what He expects of us. His word says, "Cast your cares upon Him for He cares for you".

God is such an amazing Father that He gives us 'shepherds after His own heart'. He puts leaders in place to direct us along the path that leads to spiritual growth and empowerment. After all, what we go through is merely preparing us for who our Father has purposed us to be. Therefore like a caring parent, He has set up careful facilitators to teach and instruct us in a Godly manner. Our role is then to humble ourselves and be open to wise counsel.

God equips us with wise counsel so that we don't fall prey to the enemy or become a victim of unbelief, deceit or doubt when our minds are crowded. He equips us with Godly instruction so that we may condition our minds and bring ourselves into alignment with His purpose for our lives.

"The way of a fool is right in his own eyes: but he that hearkeneth unto counsel is wise."
Proverbs 12:15

Of course we can hear from God ourselves but as human beings it is common to be misled by emotions and lack of experience. Just as God has used trials to prepare you to follow His will for you is how He has prepared others to be beacons of light in your time of need. They too have been through trials, they have been chastened and reproved just like God's people in the Bible.

Trust in the counsel that the Lord thy God sends to you. He knows that as earthly beings there will be times when we will need a companion. So He is gracious enough to prepare those that walk in His light to share wisdom and knowledge with us while molding us into our purpose.

Do not be deceived, He is not the God of confusion and will not send forth instruction that stirs up anger. This is where we are fooled when we receive advice from family and friends who are not spiritual and therefore allow emotions to lead their thoughts. God's ways are not like ours, He prepares a path for you beside still waters so that you may find rest and peace in your time of trouble.

"Get wisdom, get understanding: forget it not; neither decline from the words of my mouth. Forsake her not, and she shall preserve thee: love her, and she shall keep thee. Wisdom is the principal thing; therefore get wisdom: and with all thy getting get understanding. Exalt her, and she shall promote thee: she shall bring thee to honour, when thou dost embrace her. She shall give to thine head an ornament of grace: a crown of glory shall she deliver to thee."
Proverbs 4:5-9

What the Spirit of the Lord spoke to my heart

What the Spirit of the Lord spoke to my heart

"We must love in the midst of our trials, by extending grace and having the will to forgive. This is hard when the problems we face show us the total opposite."

Chapter 15

Kill Them With Love

———

"A new command I give you: Love one another. As I have loved you, so you must love one another."

The Lord would have us to communicate through love, in truth and with a calm spirit.

I must admit that in the heat of the moment our flesh may find a way to surpass our spirit and act swiftly without second thought. However, it is our duty to become so spiritually engulfed that we are empowered by the Lord to handle things with a heart of love.

"Above all, love each other deeply, because love covers over a multitude of sins."

The Bible teaches us that we can change the narrative of a situation by showing love, ultimately we can save a soul by showing love. At times, this may not be received with the same purity of heart that it is given. None the less, we are encouraged to do our best to sow good seeds, as God has purposed us to be His light in the earth, drawing all to Him by showing His perfect love.

This is by far the most difficult test I have received. For me, it felt like a sacrifice of self, like I was settling or lowering my standards, like I was rolling over or being passive. It is vital to stand up for ourselves and let our voices be heard. However, we must allow ourselves to be led by the Holy Spirit, so that we do so with love and grace. This may mean walking away so that our emotions do not get the best of us. At times, we may have to bite our tongues and not answer, or delete the rant and respond peaceably. We may be inclined to own our responsibilities or apologize for our wrongs.

Pride would cause us to feel like we did not handle the situation correctly, if we do not win. Do not be deceived, our goals on earth are not for flesh to win, but for the light of God to shine through us, drawing men to Him.

3 John 1:2-8 reminds us that it is the will of God that we prosper and be in good health. It further teaches us that as disciples we must be witnesses of truth and love, so that God's people may see that we are fellow helpers of the truth. We

must love in the midst of our trials, by extending grace and having the will to forgive. This is hard when the problems we face show us the total opposite. However, remember that once you are born again in Christ, you are in the world; but not of the world. You are set apart, you are peculiar, you are chosen to be God's light on earth.

1 Peter 2:9 "But you are a chosen people, a royal priesthood, a holy nation, God's special possession, that you may declare the praises of him who called you out of darkness into his wonderful light."

I am in no way encouraging you to settle or accept verbal or physical abuse. I am encouraging you to seek guidance from the Holy Spirit so that you respond in love, sowing a good seed that may ultimately achieve deliverance, favor, mercy or grace for you, or those in your bloodline. This may mean to leave peaceably and not return, it may mean to stand still and allow God to fight for you. Whatever the circumstance, I encourage you to "be wise as a serpent and harmless as a dove". You can rest assured that when you yield to the Holy Spirit, acting in the precepts of the Lord our father, He will make a way of escape for you from the hand of the enemy.

"Love is patient, love is kind. It does not envy, it does not boast, it is not proud. It does not dishonor others, it is not self-seeking, it is not easily angered, it keeps no record of wrongs. Love does not delight in evil but rejoices with the truth."

1 Corinthians 13:4-6

What the Spirit of the Lord spoke to my heart

_____

_____

_____

_____

_____

_____

_____

_____

_____

_____

_____

_____

_____

_____

_____

_____

What the Spirit of the Lord spoke to my heart

_____

_____

_____

_____

_____

_____

_____

_____

_____

_____

_____

_____

_____

In loving memory of a mighty Woman of God, a Shepherd
after God's own heart and a phenomenal mentor,
confidante, counselor, leader, mother and friend.

Apostle Muriel Elaine Harris

Meet the Author

Lashaunda Dickenson Skippings is a God-fearing wife and mother of two. She is a proud Turks and Caicos Islander that highly esteems the laws of God above all else, working in all capacities as unto God and not men.

She holds a Diploma in Special Education and a Bachelor's Degree in Educational Assessment and Instructional Planning. She is currently pursuing a Master's Degree in Educational Leadership. In doing her best to walk in God's will for her life, Lashaunda has made major strides in children's ministry. She is a beacon of God's light sharing peace and joy in her capacity as Vice Principal of the Thelma Lightbourne Primary School in Providenciales.

Adding to her passion in training the whole child, Lashaunda co-hosts a weekly Kids Club Friday evenings under the leadership of Apostle Clayton Harris at her church home, Firm Foundation Ministries International, where children are taught and groomed in the fear of God.

Lashaunda strives to live according to Colossians 3:23, "Whatever you do, work at it with all your heart, as working for the Lord, not for human masters."

Milton Keynes UK
Ingram Content Group UK Ltd.
UKHW022204221223
434840UK00015B/650